D0408331

Footprints

along the pathway of life

Introduction

Though our pathway through life takes many unexpected twists and turns, God's presence is a constant we can count on during our journey of faith. May the Scriptures and reflections in this short book strengthen and encourage you as you trace God's footprints along the pathway of your life.

S. M. H.

Footprints

BY MARGARET FISHBACK POWERS

One night I dreamed a dream.
I was walking along the beach
with my Lord.
Across the dark sky flashed
scenes from my life.
For each scene, I noticed two sets
of footprints in the sand,
one belonging to me and one
to my Lord.

When the last scene of my life
shot before me
I looked back at the footprints
in the sand.
There was only one set of footprints.
I realized that this was at the
lowest and saddest times of my life.
This always bothered me
and I questioned the Lord
about my dilemma.

'Lord, You told me when I
decided to follow You,
You would walk and talk with
me all the way.
But I'm aware that during
the most troublesome
times of my life there is only
one set of footprints.
I just don't understand why, when
I needed You most,
You leave me.'

He whispered, 'My precious child,
I love you and will never leave you,
never, ever, during your
trials and testings.
When you saw only one
set of footprints
it was then that I carried you.'

Spiritual Beginnings

Journeys often begin with excitement, anticipation, and joy. Smiles and laughter herald long-awaited vacations. Laden with baggage and sundries, we rush out the door to begin our new adventures.

Our spiritual journey often begins this way, too. Anticipation and wonderment accompany our fledgling steps of faith. The joys we find as we walk with God hurry us along the road to greater love, increased faith, and a closer relationship with Him.

—∾—

THE LORD IS GOOD
TO THOSE WHO WAIT FOR HIM,
TO THE SOUL WHO SEEKS HIM.

LAMENTATIONS 3:25, NKJV

Whatever your stance in life, have faith in God. Pray without ceasing. And give thanks for everything. Whether His providence is obscure or clear, it is always at work in your life— full of love, and right in the end. [For] the tears of life belong to the interlude, not the finale, of your story.

ALICE HUFF

THE SALVATION GOD OFFERS US
IS NOT ONLY FOR OUR FUTURE BENEFIT,
BUT FOR OUR DAY-TO-DAY NEEDS
IN THE PRESENT. HE IS AN
EVER-PRESENT HELP IN TIMES OF
TROUBLE. DAILY RELY ON HIM FOR
PEACE AND DIRECTION—
HE IS YOUR REFUGE AND STRENGTH.

GOD'S LITTLE LESSONS ON LIFE FOR MOM

To seek God is not difficult for the earnest soul, for He has left us countless clues to His presence—within us in conscience, behind us in history, around us in the best people we know, in our hands in His word,

before us in the heart's resilient
hopefulness, and plainest of all in the
ever-accessible Christ. God may not
always be obvious, but He is there:
discernible, knowable, reachable,
dependable, and ever welcoming.

AUTHOR UNKNOWN

I will walk among
you and be your God,
and you shall be
My people.

LEVITICUS 26:12, NKJV

If the blind put their hand in God's,
they find their way more surely
than those who see but have not
faith or purpose.

Helen Keller

[W]herever a man walks
faithfully in the ways that God
has marked out for him, Providence,
as the Christian says, . . .
will be on that man's side.

Henry Ward Beecher

The LORD is my shepherd;
I shall not want. He maketh me to lie
down in green pastures: he leadeth
me beside the still waters. He restoreth
my soul: he leadeth me in the paths
of righteousness for his name's sake.
Yea, though I walk through the
valley of the shadow of death, I will
fear no evil: for thou art with me;
thy rod and thy staff they comfort me.

Thou preparest a table before me
in the presence of mine enemies:
thou anointest my head with oil;
my cup runneth over. Surely goodness
and mercy shall follow me all the
days of my life: and I will dwell in
the house of the LORD for ever.

PSALM 23:1-6, KJV

All God's dealings
are full of blessing:
He is good, and doeth
good, good only, and
continually. The believer
who has taken the Lord
as his Shepherd can
assuredly say . . . :

"Surely goodness and mercy shall follow me all the days of my life." Hence we may be sure that the days of adversity, as well as days of prosperity, are full of blessings.

J. HUDSON TAYLOR

REGARD NOT MUCH WHO
IS FOR THEE OR WHO AGAINST THEE;
BUT GIVE ALL THY THOUGHT AND
CARE TO THIS, THAT GOD BE WITH
THEE IN EVERYTHING THOU DOEST.
FOR WHOM GOD WILL HELP, NO MALICE
OF MAN SHALL BE ABLE TO HURT.

THOMAS À KEMPIS

As you walk through
the valley of the unknown,
you will find the footprints
of Jesus both in front
of you and beside you.

CHARLES STANLEY

Who walks with God in just
and generous ways
With humble heart, His chief
demand obeys. . . .
From strength to strength
they journey, minds content,
Their wings like eagles',
and their hearts not faint.

AUTHOR UNKNOWN

In all His dispensations God is at work for our good. In prosperity He tries our gratitude; in mediocrity, our contentment; in misfortune, our submission; in darkness, our faith; under temptation, our steadfastness; and at all times, our obedience and trust in Him.

S. M. H.

Life is confusing at times,
and my perception of
God's way will fade.
But ... He who is the
Branch carefully guards
my path, even on the
most treacherous climb.

DEBI GROUT

We walk by faith,
not by sight.

2 Corinthians 5:7, nasb

Our gracious God
not only leads us in
the way of mercy,
but he prepares our path
before us, providing
for all our wants even
before they occur.

CHARLES SPURGEON

God does not reveal his plan,
he reveals himself. He comes to us
as warmth when we are cold,
fellowship when we are alone,
strength when we are weak,

peace when we are troubled,
courage when we are afraid,
songs when we are sad, and
bread when we are hungry.

BOB BENSON

He leads us on
By paths we do not know;
Upwards He leads us,
though our steps be slow;
Though oft we faint and
falter on the way,
Though storms and darkness
oft obscure the day,
Yet, when the clouds are gone,
We know He leads us on.

HIRAM O. WILEY

As God has said:
"I will dwell in them
And walk among them.
I will be their God,
And they shall be
My people."

2 Corinthians 6:16, nkjv

Thou, my everlasting portion,
More than friend or life to me;
All along my pilgrim journey,
Saviour, let me walk with Thee.
Close to Thee, close to Thee;
Close to Thee, close to Thee;
All along my pilgrim journey,
Saviour, let me walk with Thee.

FANNY J. CROSBY,
hymn

Only One Traveler

Photographs of our vacations serve as reminders of the sights and scenes along our journeys away from home. Many of these photographs include a friend or family member—someone who shared this memorable experience with us.

Our spiritual journeys are blessed when shared with others, too. A word of encouragement, a smile to brighten another's day, a favorite Bible verse shared with a discouraged friend, a prayer offered for another—all these things can make our own journey of faith much easier.

Yet there are times when we seem to travel through life alone. Times of grief, sadness, confusion. Though people might be all around us, our alone-ness is all encompassing. In those times we may wonder, *Where is God?*

Where can I go from Thy Spirit?
Or where can I flee from Thy presence?
If I ascend to heaven, Thou art there;
If I make my bed in Sheol,
behold, Thou art there.
If I take the wings of the dawn,
If I dwell in the remotest part of the sea,
Even there Thy hand will lead me,
And Thy right hand will lay hold of me.

PSALM 139:7–10, NASB

If the Lord be with us,

we have no cause of fear:

His eye is upon us,

His arm over us,

His ear open to our prayer—His grace sufficient, His promise unchangeable.

JOHN NEWTON

The love of God quite as often
withholds the view of the entire
distance of the winding path through
life. He reveals it to us step by step,
and from corner to corner.
Hence it is necessary to trust Him
to lead, for He can see around
the bend in the road. He knows what
lies ahead, and whether we can cope
with the situation now or later.

He consults our wants, not our
wishes, like a wise and loving Father.
His corners are not the end of the way.
Corners discipline faith, teach us
patience to walk step by step,
and fit us for blessings.
Because our vision is limited,
it causes us to continually
seek His guidance.

MRS. CHARLES E. COWMAN

Believe God's love and power
more than you believe your own
feelings and experiences. Your Rock
is Christ, and it is not the rock
that ebbs and flows but the sea.

SAMUEL RUTHERFORD

Never doubt in the
dark what God told
you in the light.

V. RAYMOND EDMAN

If we want to live intimately
with Jesus, we will need to develop
our skills. Be humble and peaceable,
and Jesus will be with you.
Be devout and quiet, and Jesus
will reside with you . . .
If discouraging and unpleasant

days come your way, don't be
despondent or defeated. Stand strong
in God and bear whatever you
must to the glory of Jesus Christ.
For after winter, summer comes.
After night, day returns.
After a storm, calm is restored.

THOMAS À KEMPIS

So shield my faith, that
I may never doubt Thee,
For I must fall, if e'er
I walk without Thee.

FRANCIS QUARLES

Because you have made the LORD,
who is my refuge,
Even the Most High, your
dwelling place,
No evil shall befall you,
Nor shall any plague come
near your dwelling;

For He shall give His angels
charge over you,
To keep you in all your ways.
In their hands they shall bear you up,
Lest you dash your foot against a stone.

PSALM 91:9–12, NKJV

The steps of a good man
are ordered by the LORD,
And He delights in his way.
Though he fall, he shall
not be utterly cast down;
For the LORD upholds
him with His hand.

PSALM 37:23–24, NKJV

[A]biding in Christ is just meant for the weak, and so beautifully suited to their feebleness. It is not the doing of some great thing, and does not demand that we first lead a very holy and devoted life. No, it is simply weakness entrusting itself to a Mighty One to be kept—the unfaithful one casting self on One who is altogether trustworthy and true.

ANDREW MURRAY

I will lift up mine eyes unto the hills, from whence cometh my help. My help cometh from the Lord, which made heaven and earth. He will not suffer thy foot to be moved: he that keepeth thee will not slumber. Behold, he that keepeth Israel shall neither slumber nor sleep.

Psalm 121:1-4 KJV

O how sweet to walk in this pilgrim way,

Leaning on the everlasting arms;

O, how bright the path grows
from day to day

Leaning on the everlasting arms.

Leaning on Jesus, leaning on Jesus,

Safe and secure from all alarms;

Leaning on Jesus, leaning on Jesus,

Leaning on the everlasting arms.

ELISHA A. HOFFMAN,
hymn

The Truth of
God's Promise

Small children are fearless when
holding tightly to the hand of a
trusted adult.

Toddlers will try faltering steps; preschoolers will attempt to ride tricycles. Even kindergarteners will agree to forgo training wheels as long as a trusted hand holds tightly to the back of the seat.

God provides that trusted hand for us in our daily walk of faith. When we face the unknowns of life, He holds out His hand of reassurance to grasp our own. When we roll over life's rough-hewn road of suffering, He offers His arm of strength to carry us through. And, when it seems we must go on alone without the aid of friends, family, or work, God offers us the added promise of His abiding presence.

He shall feed his flock like a shepherd: he shall gather the lambs with his arm, and carry them in his bosom, and shall gently lead those that are with young.

ISAIAH 40:11, KJV

WE WILL NEVER BE SATISFIED
WITH ANYTHING LESS—EACH DAY,
EACH HOUR, OR EACH MOMENT
IN CHRIST, THROUGH THE POWER
OF THE HOLY SPIRIT—
THAN WALKING WITH GOD.

H. C. G. MOULE

[I]t is not only after the future thou must aspire; thou must aspire to see the glory of thy past. Thou must find the glory of that way by which thy God has led thee, and be able even of thy sorrow to say, "This was the gate of heaven!"

GEORGE MATHESON

I DO NOT ASK THAT I MAY WALK
ONLY ON SMOOTHLY
    TRODDEN GRASS,
NOR EVER CLIMB THE
    MOUNTAIN'S HEIGHT
AND TREMBLING, THROUGH
    ITS DANGERS PASS;
I ONLY ASK, ON ROCKS OR SAND,
THE SURE UPHOLDING OF
    THY HAND.

ANNIE JOHNSON FLINT

Behind every prayer and behind
every promise, there is God …
And if he exists at all, we know
he must be enough … [N]othing else
really matters—neither creeds,
nor ceremonies, nor doctrines, nor
dogmas. God is; God is unselfish;
and God is enough!

Hannah Whitall Smith

The LORD, He is the
One who goes before you.
He will be with you,
He will not leave you
nor forsake you; do not
fear nor be dismayed.

DEUTERONOMY 31:8, NKJV

We *can* trust God, not just
in his grand design for our lives and
the eventual happy ending to the
story, but in his promise that we
will have a companion in every
circumstance, however fearful.
Jesus' last words to his disciples...

were, "Surely I am with you always, to the very end of the age" (Matthew 28:20, NIV). To the end of our lives, to the end of time, we are not alone, and we can "fear not."

BRUCE LARSON

[A]s we make repeated efforts to
realize the presence of God,
it will become increasingly real to us.
And as the habit grows upon us,
when alone in a room, or
when treading the grass of some
natural woodland temple, or when
pacing the stony street—

in the silence of the night,
or amid the teeming crowds
of daylight—we shall often
find ourselves whispering the
words, "Thou art near;
Thou are here, O Lord."

F. B. MEYER

A small boy liked to walk
with his father through the fields
and neighboring pastures behind
their farm. At first the little fellow
gripped his father's index finger,
but found that whenever he stumbled
on something, his grip would slip
and down he'd go into the dirt.
This happened several times.
Finally the little boy said,

"Daddy, I think if *you* would hold *my* hand, I wouldn't fall." The father did as his son requested, and though the little fellow stumbled a bit, he never hit the ground. So, too, in our walk with our Heavenly Father, we must let Him hold on to us. We may stumble a bit, but He will never let us fall.

S. M. H.

For just as the sufferings
of Christ are ours in
abundance, so also our
comfort is abundant
through Christ.

2 CORINTHIANS 1:5, NASB

The truth really is that his care
is infinitely superior to any possibilities
of human care; and that he, who
counts the very hairs of our heads,
and suffers not a sparrow to fall
without him, takes note of the
minutest matters that can affect the
lives of his children, and regulates them
all according to his own perfect will.

HANNAH WHITALL SMITH

[I]T IS AS WE, THROUGH GRACE, YIELD A HEARTY AND HAPPY OBEDIENCE TO OUR FATHER'S STATUTES AND JUDGMENTS THAT WE TREAD THE BRIGHT PATHWAY OF LIFE, AND ENTER INTO THE REALITY OF ALL THAT GOD HAS TREASURED UP FOR US IN CHRIST.

C. H. MACKINTOSH

"For behold I am coming
and I will dwell in
your midst,"
declares the LORD.

ZECHARIAH 2:10, NASB

Though I walk in the midst
of trouble, you preserve my life;
you stretch out your hand against
the anger of my foes, with your
right hand you save me. The LORD
will fulfill [his purpose] for me;
your love, O LORD, endures forever.

PSALM 138:7–8, NIV

THERE IS NEVER A TIME WHEN WE
MAY NOT *HOPE IN GOD!*
WHATEVER THE NECESSITIES,
HOWEVER GREAT OUR DIFFICULTIES,
AND THOUGH TO ALL APPEARANCES
HELP IS IMPOSSIBLE, YET OUR BUSINESS
IS TO *HOPE IN GOD*, AND IT WILL BE
FOUND THAT IT IS NOT IN VAIN.

GEORGE MUELLER

When we walk with the Lord
in the light of His Word,
What a glory He sheds on our way!
While we do His good will
He abides with us still,
And with all who will trust and obey.

Then in fellowship sweet we
will sit at His feet,
Or we'll walk by His side
in the way;

What He says we will do,
where He sends we will go—
Never fear, only trust and obey.

Trust and obey, for there's
no other way
To be happy in Jesus,
But to trust and obey.

JOHN H. SAMMIS,
hymn

There is nothing in the world as delightful as a continual walk with God. Only those who have experienced it can comprehend it. And yet I do not recommend that you seek it solely because it is so enjoyable. Do it because of love, and because it is what God wants... Practice... the presence of God.

BROTHER LAWRENCE

Photo Credits

Page 5: © Bill Ross/Corbis
Pages 14-15: © Geoffrey Clifford/The Image Bank
Pages 23, 70: © James Randklev/The Image Bank
Pages 30-31: © Stuart Westmorland/The Image Bank
Pages 38-39: © Darrell Gulin/The Image Bank
Page 47: © Dave Schiefelbein/The Image Bank
Pages 54-55: © Michael Townsend/The Image Bank
Pages 62-63: © Kaz Mori/The Image Bank
Pages 76-77: © Silvestre Machado/Photonica

Background images throughout:
Pages 6-7, etc. © Darrell Gulin/The Image Bank
Pages 10-11, etc. © Michael Townsend/
                                    The Image Bank
Pages 12-13, etc. © Gary Braasch/The Image Bank

Scripture quotations marked NKJV are taken from
The New King James Version of the Bible.
Copyright © 1979, 1980, 1982, 1994 by
Thomas Nelson, Inc., Publishers. Used by permission.

Scripture quotations marked NASB are taken
from the *New American Standard Bible.*
Copyright © 1960, 1962, 1963, 1968,
1971, 1972, 1973, 1975, 1977
by The Lockman Foundation. Used by permission.

Scripture quotations marked NIV are taken from
the *Holy Bible, New International Version.*
Copyright © 1973, 1978, 1984 by International
Bible Society. Used by permission of
Zondervan Publishing House. All rights reserved.

Scripture quotations marked KJV are taken from
the *King James Version* of the Bible.

Excerpt on page 13 taken from
God's Little Lessons on Life for Mom.
Copyright © 1999 by Honor Books, Tulsa, OK.
Used by permission.